G000244499

When You Haven't Got a Prayer

LION
Giftlines

*This little book is for the people of
St. Luke's Church in Holloway, London
where many of its prayers
first left earth for heaven.*

When You Haven't Got a Prayer

Martin Wroe

With illustrations by
Nick Newman

... AND HERE'S ONE I CREATED EARLIER

Published by
Lion Publishing plc
Sandy Lane West, Oxford, England
ISBN 0 7459 3696 2
Albatross Books Pty Ltd
PO Box 320, Sutherland, NSW 2232, Australia
ISBN 0 7324 1575 6

First edition 1997
10 9 8 7 6 5 4 3 2 1 0

A catalogue record for this book is available
from the British Library

Printed and bound in Singapore

Most people pray sometimes. Some people often. Occasionally it's easy, mostly it's not. The Apostle Paul told the early Christians to 'pray without ceasing'. I'm nearly there—I can pray badly without ceasing.

This is a book of prayers I have prayed, many of which started life in the church I'm part of. The prayers I'd come across previously had so much faith in them there was no room for my doubts. I started writing my own for when I didn't have a prayer.

These are prayers to a God who cradles our lives in his safe hands, but seems to go all shy and retiring when asked about it. Or maybe they're simply prayers from someone hard of hearing.

Good prayer requires thought, but in its finest moments prayer transcends the mind, like a child splashing in the water who suddenly realizes she is swimming. Have a splash.

Martin Wroe

Like . . .

What are you like?

Like a man who coughs
while hiding,
said the mystic
(talking like one).

Like a burglar in the dark
stepping on a loose floorboard,
the smell of frying bacon wafting
from an unseen window,
a bird rustling her clothes in
motionless branches,
the opening bars of a song you know
... before you can name it
 a sneeze so shocking it clears the head.
 the fleeting, embarrassed eye-contact
... opening the soul,
 a rumour so strange that maybe it's true.

What are you like?

The momentary intuition,
the blink of the other,
the brilliant thought
too fine for words
that slips through the brain cells
... only its recall can be recalled.

What are you like?

Cough.
Cough.

Noise

They say you're available
on certain conditions.
Quiet ones.
That if I can find an air of tranquillity
it carries that still small voice.

But I don't do quiet,
stillness.
I am not tranquil except when I am asleep
and then I am not available
as far as I know.

So,
what's the chance of a still big voice
in the noise,
of hearing you in the roaring traffic,
the screaming meal-time,
the crowded train,
the supermarket queue,
the smoky, throbbing bar?

I know that time you weren't
in the fire,
the storm.
But everyone's different.
Maybe Elijah was better at quiet.

You're usually quiet.
I'm usually wired.
If I try for your silence,
perhaps you could try for my noise.

Your place or mine?
I know they say you're in
the country,
but maybe we could meet in town....

Knock, Knock

Is there anyone there?

This is the invisible question mark we all carry
balancing on top of our heads.
Is there anyone there?
Out there, in there, somewhere,
anywhere?

We race through our three score years and ten,
the road stretching endlessly ahead.
We don't need signs,
we're immortal,
we take the ride of our life.

Some say they've seen signs,
sitting round a table a glass moves,
someone else saw a blind man healed,
even a dead person raised.
Someone said they died and met their mother,
who said it wasn't time yet,
they must go back, finish the washing up.
Some say they heard the whisper of a speech
telling them how their future looks
jumping from a verse in the Book.

Some say they've seen wonders,
a flower straining wide for the
touch of the morning sun,
water pouring like rush-hour over the
Niagara Falls,
stars hanging in the sky, winking like
a god with a nervous tic.

Some say they've seen signs and wonders,
people babbling in foreign tongues,
crying like babies, laughing like hyenas,
the Spirit falls on them, like a pissed mugger on
a backstreet, leaves them rolling on the floor,
moves drunkenly on to crack the joke with
another.

The songwriter said,
these are the days of miracles and wonders,
but most times the signs are not so clear.
Most days, we're alone,
no voice from the heavens.
The pages of your book are silent.

Then, God,
you're like a man painting street signs
in a strange language,
you're like the child showing her parents
her drawing of a cow,
which looks more like East Anglia.
We can't understand the signs...
and sometimes it seems like
you're playing with us,
that you don't want to be found out,
that you're embarrassed or shy...
Even Jesus worked his wonders
and told the people to shut their mouths.

What's your problem with doing something
obvious for a change,
a jokey sunset at lunchtime, maybe,
or a giraffe that finds a voice to proclaim a
cure for the AIDS virus?
maybe vaporizing the world's weapons supplies
all at once.

Go on,
give us a sign...

But some days, I turn and see you.
For a second you're there, grinning,
like maybe you were glad to have been
caught in the act of being a God,
but not glad enough to hang around
showing off...

Other days, I've seen your signs and wonders
in the skin-cracked face of an Indian saint
wiping saliva from the lips of a dying nobody,
in the nervous ink
signing the impossible peace treaty,
in the bomber giving up his semtex,
handing in her guns,
in the child born to the family who'd given up,
in the loving-kindness of the mother
of a brain-damaged child,
in the kindness of a stranger
offering his fags around,
in the slow jittery words
of someone asking forgiveness...
in the gentle touch of a lover
in the warm, accepting dark...
in the mysterious sip of the blood-wine
in a Communion cup.

But these signs are hard to read.
Their lettering faint, almost rubbed out.
Sometimes the signs are blown over
on the roadside.
We drive by, hooked
on the wonder of your world,
oblivious to its sponsor.
This wonder-full so common
we think it wonder-empty,
these signs mundane,
their words a blur,
their meaning lost in a thousand
interpretations.

Is there anyone there?
Perhaps,
for those with eyes to see,
who slow down,
stop,
get out and struggle
through the roadside overgrowth
to another path,
uncovering another dilapidated sign,
sitting in deep silence,
... a place where we'll find you,
lover and beloved,
sign and destiny.

This sign is a wonder.
I am the way,
says the sign,
I am the way.

if I stopped

if I stopped

if I was quiet for a minute
if I was calm
if I was silent
if I was still

if I turned everyone down
if I switched everything off
if I ceased looking everywhere all at once
if I was silent
if I was still

if I stayed home
if I didn't pick up the phone
if I was out even when I was in
if I was silent
if I was still...

if I slowed
right
down

if I simply sat
here
there
anywhere

if I stood on my head
and emptied out the contents

if I stopped

would you be there
would you speak to me
would I be able to hear
would I know it was you
would it be worth it?

if I stopped
would it be long enough?

if I was silent
would I hear anything?

if I heard something
would I know it was you?

if I did
would I be interested?

if I was
would I stop again?

Gone

It is now later than when this sentence started
... and earlier than when it ends.
The sentence was full of it...
but it's not made of letters,
and you can't ever see it.
It passes.
It is passing.
It has passed.

It waits for no one.
It is here today and here tomorrow.
It will only be completely past when all the
tomorrows have been completely used up.
There is more of it than of anything else...
but there is never enough of it.
It shall be.
It is.
It was.
Look, there it goes... now.

You can run out of it
and be pressed for it.
You can take it off
and have it quietly.

You can travel in it,
to the edge of your imagination.

It is quietly but ever present.
It does not tick...
or tock.
You can't stop it or speed it up.
It will trap you, catch you, control you.
There is a time for everything,
because without everything
there is no time at all.

We are all of us doing time,
but none of us have time to notice.
Only those who take time
can tell the time,
understand the time.
It is a trickster with a god-complex.
It believes it runs us.
And when there is time for nothing,
your universe has broken down,
your timer needs re-setting,
a visit to a watchsmith,
... if you can find time.

There is a place where they watch time,
where one day—the last day—
a voice will call, 'Time gentlemen please'.
Someone wearing rubber gloves will go around
carefully picking up all the hours and minutes
and seconds.
She will pop them in a large chest of drawers,
next to a wardrobe which is hung full of weeks
and months.
The word *time* will enter the dictionary in the
Offensive Words section,
joining *rush*,
busy
and *later*.

The trickster will be exposed,
the illusion undone.
Everything will become clear
and a day will be as a thousand years.

Here is the day

Here is the day,
travelling into my eyes
at the speed of light,
stopping for nothing, no one.
My mind runs.
My time runs out.

Here is *your* day.
Take it.
You'll have to be quick,
quicker than the speed of light.
From here on
I'll be taking it back,
every hour, minute, second.

By the end of your day
I will have taken it all back for myself.

Here is the day.
Quick
God
quick.

Take it. It's yours.

Forget

We give thanks for peace,
Which we forget until war approaches.
We give thanks for friendship,
Which we forget until we fall out.
We give thanks for sight,
Which we forget until we cannot see.
We give thanks for faith,
Which we forget until we lose it.
We give thanks for breath,
Which we forget until we remind ourselves.
We give thanks for ourselves,
Which we need no reminding of.
We give thanks to God,
Without whom we can neither forget
nor remember.

Churches

Dear God,
We give thanks for all churches everywhere,
for full ones and empty ones,
noisy ones and quiet ones,
silly churches and clever ones,
high churches and short ones,
fat churches and thin ones,
Spirit-filled and Spirit-seeking,
right ones and wrong ones,
and those that alternate.
We give thanks for vicars, ministers and priests
and all who dress up on Sunday,
preachers and listeners,
singers and sung to,
pray-ers and prayed for
and those who live to answer prayers.
We give thanks for people
who belong in church
and those who don't,
for people who know why they go
and people who wish they'd never been,
for those who come annually
and those who come daily,
those at the front and those at the back.

We give thanks for those who see you clearly
and those who don't notice you
as you sit down beside them.
We give thanks for all churches everywhere.

Touch

if we could glimpse you passing by this week
if we could hear you through the crowd
if we could shake you and wake you
when the storm sets in
if we could touch the hem of your garment
then we would be blessed

if we could hear you were spinning tales
in the next town
if we could send for you
when our loved ones died
if we could read the nails on your palms
if we could touch the hem of your garment
then we would be blessed

if we could meet you by accident down the shops
if we could climb a tree to see you
if we could ask you back for a drink
if we could touch the hem of your garment
then we would be blessed

if we could follow you balancing on the water
if we could visit you after night has fallen
if we could take you to the hospital
to see our sick ones

if we could touch the hem of your garment
then we would be blessed

if we could see you in the lonely
and the hungry
if we could sell all we have and follow you
if we could even stay awake and pray
if we could touch the hem of your garment
then we would be blessed

Flesh of our flesh

Dear God
When were you last slapped,
hard in the face,
out of the blue,
so you were stunned,
had pins and needles,
lost your sense of being for a second
and then watched your skin swell, darken, run
red
... and stretch to its limits?

When did you last hold a baby up to
your own face, God,
smell the warm body,
touch the innocent skin,
know the life pass between you, with no words?

Do you have feelings too, God?
Do things touch you?
Are you spirit or are you substance,
for real or only ether-real,
are you there or everywhere?
If we reached out and touched you
would our hands pass right through
... your elusive, divine self?

What about any distinguishing characteristics?
What colour are you, God?
How's your eyesight,
what's your body like,
would we spot you in a crowd,
would we stare at you for some disability?

How many senses have you got, God,
five, six, eighteen, ninety-four?
And your sense of touch,
is your handshake firm as a vice
or slippery as an eel?
What do you smell of, God?
Anything in particular,
the universe, is it,
planets, oceans, space, skies?

If it's true that your Spirit is always willing
... is your flesh ever weak?
And if the Word was made flesh,
are you flesh of our flesh,
bone of our bone?

Is that you there, meek and mild,
meanly wrapped in swaddling clothes?
Is that you, Baby J,

Word of the Father,
now in flesh appearing,
is that you, screaming as you arrive
like the rest of us,
screaming at the shock of the new,
the shock of the cold and the old and the broken?
Is that you,
slipping clumsily out from between
a Virgin's legs,
covered in blood and gunge and straw,
when moments before,
you had been covered in glory?
Tied to the mother of God by stringy flesh,
sucking for your very life on a woman's breast
... what a come-down.

And is that someone slapping your bum,
a world-first,
God gets a thrashing,
God gets to feel flesh on flesh
and it makes him cry?

Still, at least you had an audience,
cows, was it, or maybe a goat or two?
Did they look on in awe and wonder,
were the cattle lowing a bit,
or were they a smelly nuisance?

But 'little Lord Jesus no crying he makes'.
Well, that doesn't sound right.
The thing about flesh is that it makes you cry;
for better or worse, you've got to cry.
'Who is he in yonder stall
at whose feet the shepherds fall?'
Did they fall?
Did they recognize you up close,
did they know that it was you, God,
starkers, in the flesh,
or were they just intrigued by
the heavenly host
and that funny star?

And did the flesh inconvenience
and annoy and anger you,
like it does the rest of us,
your fleshy creatures?
Did your nose run green,
your skin flake or bruise red,
Did your breath catch with asthma
in that smelly barn,
your chest tighten in fear?
were you irritated by flies and gnats
(ones you had made earlier),
... or did they show some respect?

And later on, what did you do about
your fleshly lusts?
And, just out of interest, where, on earth,
did you go for your private movements
—are there miraculously fertile plants
there today,
trees with roots for miles
and branches into the heavens
forever bearing fruit
... or are those places
where the divine squatted in squalor with his
lowly creatures,
and wiped his bum with leaves,
just like any other place?

When you were tired,
when it all was going wrong,
when your friends misunderstood,
lost interest,
wandered off,
did you think,
'What did I get into this body-business for?'
swapping spirit for flesh,
swapping omnipresence for being somewhere
... in particular?
Did you feel trapped in that body,
or didn't you know what it had been like

before you became body?
When you were in-carnate
... did you recall what it was like
being out-carnate?
Flesh doesn't fly, usually,
flesh can't be in more than one place at a time,
flesh is limited, awkward.
Did you ever notice it,
did you wonder at the restrictions of
the body corporeal,
or were you just one of us,
God Inc.?

Did the flesh exhilarate you,
excite you,
did you run and laugh and fall,
did you sweat and wrestle and argue
and were you grateful to live
on earth
a human
in flesh
to be one of us?

He was little, weak and helpless,
tears and smiles like us he knew,
and he feeleth for our sadness,
and he shareth in our gladness.

And how's your body now,
do you wear a halo, or a crown,
is it of gold, or is it of thorns,
are there marks on your palms,
have you got blood on the side of your shirt still?

Jesus of the body, of the flesh,
Jesus of the teeth and hair and toenails,
welcome to the body, God
and thank you for taking it,
for putting flesh on the bones of
our skeletal lives,
thank you, Jesus, for becoming body among us,
that veiled in flesh Godhead we see.

Flesh is all we have
but, as *you* know now,
flesh is not all we are.

Act of love

I was wondering today
if you'd ever fallen in love.

Did you ever even kiss anyone?
Not a holy kiss, one of those religious things
lost in a self-conscious embrace,
a kiss with no visible bodily contact.
No, what about a kiss of desire,
a kiss that said 'I'm going to swallow you
whole,' an unselfconscious kiss with four lips
and then no lips?

You get some big scenes at weddings,
obviously,
they usually use your book,
but what do you know about weddings
(apart from the wine routine),
about men and women,
shivers up your spine and
action in your trousers?

You had women friends, women who loved you,
fancied you even... but as far as anyone knows
you never got engaged or married.

Did you ever get asked out
('Jesus, you doing anything Saturday night?')?
Did you ever see someone across the street and
feel the hairs on the back of your neck
bristling,
ever hold her hand and feel like a millionaire,
ever exchange knowing glances that nobody
except her knew about?
Was there ever a time when your heart was so
tight with love it threatened to attack you
(or were you always like that about everyone)?

What do you know about love, God?

Some say you're sexless or anti-sex.
It's for making babies not fun,
for expressing the life-force,
not for expressing forever and ever.
Even the organization that named itself after
you... your bride... your lover... some parts
don't let their priests marry.
Do you care as little about physical love?

When you created the universe and
her million sisters,
was that you inventing friendship,
... two's company, one isn't?

That opening seven cosmic days was sexier
than the twentieth century.
The Big Bang before the birth of us all,
is that how you made us your children?
And are our tiny loves,
our small bangs,
grainy Polaroids of that first great
act of love?

Are you in love with us?
This feeling we have for our special others,
for our of-all-most-loved-ones,
is this the feeling you had
when you first made us all,
stepped back and said, 'It's good'?
Are we made of love, not chemicals,
our blood pumping from your heart,
no less powerful for being invisible?
Does your pulse quicken when we turn
and face you?

And is yours an unrequited love?
Are we the ones who've always got
something else on,
who are really in love with someone else,
anyone else?

Did we leave you waiting at the altar,
your dearly beloved
with the dearest love of all?

Was that love, hanging on wood by its
blue fingertips?
Your bloody Valentine,
unsigned message,
big, red heart pinned up for all,
pierced till all the big, red love drained away...

Broken heart for broken universe.

They say you spin every spider's web, every day
(the kind of obsessive, pointless detail lovers
bother with),
that a leaf doesn't fall from a tree
without you knowing.
that a person doesn't go to their grave without
you joining the mourners
in the grey drizzle.

Maybe the lives of all true lovers
are secretly fired by your own
quiet,
endless
love,
of which ours is a meek and lowly sign,
a tiny,
trembling
signal...

Have you ever been in love?

The Friday

Dear Jesus Christ
(may I call you Jesus?)
I've been thinking about your life down here,
particularly the end of it,
the last day actually,
the Friday.
Not wishing to be rude,
but exactly how much did you know?

Some say you knew everything
(that it was foretold),
which makes what you did so great.
Other say you didn't know,
which probably makes it even greater.
But if you'd known then what we know now,
would you have gone through with it?
I'm thinking of all the churches,
of Protestants and Catholics,
popes and bishops.
I'm thinking of people killing each other
after a prayer,
scarred families,
torn communities,
... you get my point.

Put it like this,
if you'd known this kingdom of yours would take
so long to show,
would you have switched strategies?

They say a week is a long time in politics,
but politics has nothing on your last week.
You came in as a king on a donkey,
did you know you'd go out a criminal on a cross?
You came talking about a kingdom of God,
did you know you'd leave in
a fancy-dress crown of thorns?
You came in with the world at your feet,
did you know you'd be leaving with the world
on your shoulders?

So, if you'd had the foresight,
like we have the hindsight,
would you have gone through with it?
You only had to deny the charges,
like Peter denied you.
Supposing you'd thrown up your arms
and called it a day, *'Alright, I admit I quite fancy
being saviour of the world but
I'm not going to die for it.'*

You could've been less ambitious,
started some kind of club instead,
no need for a whole new religion,
a *kingdom* for God's sake.
What about a small society,
with you the life President?
Did you never think,
'Well, you only live once, no point blowing it on a
technicality about whether or not I'm the Messiah...'?

Still,
it's history now; you didn't pull a fast one.
It's as if you did know what had to be done.
You took the booby prize,
the one-way trip to Golgotha.

So what were you thinking about
as you limped along to Calvary,
when every conceivable plan had gone wrong
and only the inconceivable ones were left?
I don't believe you were thinking about saving
the world,
were you?

As you lurched along the road,
the butt of bad jokes and stale fruit,
did you spare a thought for the smug smiles
on the faces of power?
Were you thinking of the disciples,
gone to ground,
or maybe the woman you'd never marry
(was there someone?),
the children you'd never have,
the bosom friends who'd suddenly
never heard of you?
Maybe you were just thinking about the nails...

Did you get angry with God
for letting it come to this?
Did you swear at him... or bottle it up
(I bet it's come out since)?

Come to think of it, for a man of faith
who wanted others to put their faith in him,
you sometimes seemed plagued with self-doubt.
Perhaps you became an atheist for a little while.
Can God become an atheist?
(Is a god with an identity crisis an agnostic,
a god who ceases to believe in himself,
an atheist?)

If you'd known about the shamefaced shambles
of that last day,
would you have gone through with it?
Did you know the Last Supper was going to be
your last supper,
a very bad Friday would go down in history
as a good Friday,
you were about to create a more effective logo
than Coca Cola,
and the most popular piece of jewellery
in history,
that your name would become a holy word
... and the commonest of swear words?

Christ, it must have been lonely,
walking that cross up the hill of the skull,
two pieces of first-century low-life
banged up on either side,
... no one left at all.
It must have been the loneliest place
in the world,
the loneliest place in history,
one person against the world,
one person for the world.

You must have thought
God had stopped believing in you.

Pilate, Herod, Barabbas...
they didn't know that as you went up
on a cross,
they were going down in history.
They didn't know much, really.
They didn't know about the third day
... and the fourth day,
about the first millennium
and the second.

I don't imagine you'd have done any different.
But I wonder,
with foresight,
if they'd have done any different
from the rest of us,
with hindsight.

The hands of God

I'm looking at my hands,
holding them up to my face.
I smell them,
taste them,
rub them against my cheek.
I know these hands better than anyone,
yet I scarcely know them at all.
On the ends of my arms
are the hands of God.

If I were you, God,
I'd change the world,
fill empty bellies,
heal broken bodies,
balance the imbalanced,
find the lost,
trip up the powerful,
brighten the miserable,
enlighten the confused.

People wonder, you know,
why you don't release the hostages,
quieten the gunfire,
stop the bombs,

why you don't get politicized,
why you don't prick the consciences
of those holding prisoners of conscience,
why you don't
topple fascist regimes,
make everyone vegetarian,
stop motorways erasing forests,
fridges erasing ozone,
why you don't end racism, sexism, ageism,
sizeism,
... atheism, obviously.

If I were you,
I'd think it was time
to do something.
I'd get my hands dirty.

If I were you, God,
I wouldn't have done things your way,
opening your hands wide for this world
only for us to split them wider,
seeing we could do with a hand
and giving us both.

There's your Spirit, of course,
Still moving over the face of the deep
and the shallow
And then there's us.
(This I would have done differently.)
We are your hands now
and we no longer nail them,
we just tie them tight,
knotted with a million excuses.

If I were you,
I'd move that Spirit on us,
change us from cynical to hopeful,
cold to warm,
indifferent to motivated,
change us into people like Jesus
uncurling our frozen fists,
spreading hands wide
despite the hammer's risk.

I suppose your way has worked,
you *have* changed the world,
but it's still hard to imagine
a place called future
where dying is history,

where the present can be seen in context,
where the random
and the chance
and the meaningless
are pieces you have fitted in a
transcendental jigsaw,
where tearducts are only used with laughter
where your hands are indistinguishable
from our hands.

Look at your hands.
Hold them up to your face,
smell them,
taste them, rub them against your cheek.
You know them better than anyone,
yet you scarcely know them at all.
On the ends of your arms
are the hands of God.

Two miracles

Dear God,
We think of some people whose spirits
we have never met,
whose hands we will never squeeze.
They look at us from our newspapers
and move before us on our TV screens.
They are across the sea
and in our living room.
We have nothing in common with them
apart from everything.
Your breath animates them like us
and now their breath is stopped...
theirs for good,
ours for a moment.
If there, why not here?
If them, why not us?
In this quiet is a sound
...the deafening crack in their interrupted lives.

This thought is for a miracle.
Turn our thinking into a prayer.
Make these thoughts make a difference.
Sit your big self down
next to those who are weeping,
listen to those who are angry.

Hold those about to break.
Kiss those who can't go on.
Show yourself to those who can see only
nothing.

And chase down justice
fast as your mercy.

This prayer is for two miracles:
turn our thoughts into prayer,
turn evil into good.

I don't believe in angels

I'll come clean with you,
I don't believe in angels.
But, for the purpose of this chat,
let's suppose I did
... a great host of the heavenly riders
bellowing out songs of praise
like the Good Book says.

Well, what kind of life is that?
I mean, where do they go
when there's no choir practice?
And if they're immortal, not having been born
and not having to die,
how come none of your great artists ever paint
them taking a drag on a fag?
If I were an immortal cherub, certain not to get
the big C,
I would.

Some folk think of angels
like UFOs,
sparks in the dark,
strange torches dipping behind clouds,
hovering above cars which then career
off roads...

I can't believe this stuff myself,
but I recall the Book talks about people
entertaining angels unawares.
You buy some bum in a shop doorway
a Big Mac and unawares
you're feeding old Gabriel.
Imagine that!
You bump into a stranger leaving the football
of a Saturday and you're giving an angel a shove.

Take a busy street, with ten thousand shoppers.
How many of them are angels?
I heard ten per cent will be gay.
What per cent will be fliers?
And which ones are they?
That man with the worry graffitied
on his forehead?
That girl pushing her baby in the buggy?
Your bus driver in the morning, maybe?

And where do they live?
How do they get these jobs?
What do they tell their friends—or their
family—do angels come out
in their late teens?
'Mum, Dad... sit down,
there's something we need to talk about.

I'm not the way I seem.
I'm different.
I've developed these wings...'

My theory goes like this.
The Book calls angels 'messengers of God',
sort of heavenly motorcycle couriers,
the original space cadets.
So what's the message God wants out now
after twenty centuries of Christianity?
Surely it's the same as the previous one,
which hasn't quite caught on.
Love against the odds,
small guy against big guy,
give out not up,
light in the dark,
last shall be first,
truth will out...
you know the kind of thing.

And you find God's messengers
where you find God's message,
the old dear helped across the busy street,
the prisoner of conscience
standing up against her torturers,
a child leaning over her friend's
bloody knee in the playground,

a man wiping sweat from the face of his lover
who has AIDS.
Schindler making his list,
that woman taking another's place in the queue
for the gas chamber,
Jesus stapled to a cross between blood and
wood when he could have cleared off home.

Don't get me wrong.
Maybe your angels are up there
with their harps and big wings and bigger hair,
but until I've seen one,
I'll settle for anyone
filling the hungry belly of another,
putting clothes on the shivering,
cooling the boiling sick,
listening to the boring.
To my mind, everyone who does this grows
invisible wings and sings in a heavenly choir.

Maybe there is angel music in the universe
that only God tunes his wireless to.
Maybe there are angels singing in the realms of
glory even now...
I don't know.
I don't believe in angels.

Imagine

So I'm just thinking to myself, right...
I'm thinking that John Lennon said,
'Imagine there's no heaven...'
But I'm thinking, 'Get lost, John—think I
might imagine there is'....

A place where the buses run on time,
and women walk safe after dark.
Where eating chocolate reduces cholesterol,
smoking is relaxing but doesn't cause cancer,
and you can't get headaches or hangovers.

I'm thinking of a place where nurses earn as
much as company chairmen,
policemen are liked but not really necessary
and teachers don't want to be anything else.
Where children run multinationals for fun
and grown-ups are sent to bed every time
they're rude.

A place where you can be busy
if you want to be,
but you can buy extra time when you need it
(from an Extra Time Shop).

A place where you can go to sleep
when you're tired,
deep, deep sleep so you wake up feeling like
you've had a life transfusion
like your life has been heated up.

I'm thinking of a place where nobody notices
their nakedness
and species aren't endangered.
Where you've got all shapes and sizes...
but no one great or small.
Where people meet you
and don't even notice your bone structure
or your colour
because they're so struck by your soul.
Where they hear your spirit not your accent
and everyone knows that everyone's only a
mere immortal.

Of course
this heaven is not a religious place.
I mean there'll be no Jehovah's Witnesses at
your door (who needs a witness when Jehovah's
down the road?)
and God won't be a rumour because he'll have
a front door.

You won't have to pray because you can talk.
There is no need for churches,
mosques or temples.
No one tells you how to live your life
because no one needs to.
There'll be no streets of gold
or pearly gates or harps,
no big dad god and little boy god
on matching thrones.
No regrets
but a place where every time you bump into a
why
you can feel a *because*.

There will still be bad language.
Words like *bomb* and *bullet* and *rape*.
There will even be the odd four-letter word
... *hate*,
for example.
But some words will not be able to be spelled
at all
... *fear*,
poverty,
pain,
death,

because these words will come from
an ancient language
no longer understood
occasionally studied but never spoken.

I'm imagining a place called heaven.
A place where you can eat chocolate
and fight heart disease,
take a long, slow drag on a fag
to cure someone of cancer,
climb through the air on wings like eagles,
run but never get tired.

G o d

God
within
and
without

God
underground and overground
everywhere and nowhere
always and never
sometimes and all times

God
inside
and
outside

God
here
with
us
now.

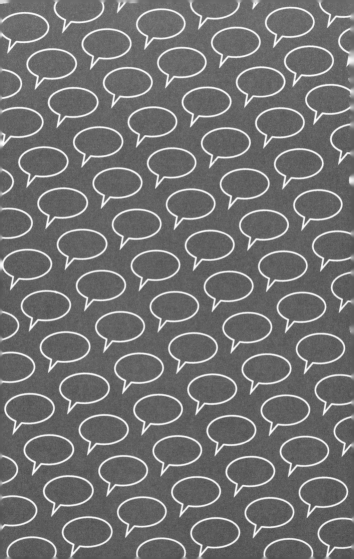